CONFESSIONS of

LOVE

CONFESSIONS of

LOVE

"If I Die never Having Loved, Then I Die Never Having Lived"
"Don't Cry Because Its Over, Smile Because It Happened"

SARAH CHEMAISSEM

BALBOA.
PRESS

A DIVISION OF HAY HOUSE

Balboa Press books may be ordered through booksellers or by contacting:

Balboa Press
A Division of Hay House
1663 Liberty Drive
Bloomington, IN 47403
www.balboapress.com
1-(877) 407-4847

Because of the dynamic nature of the Internet, any web addresses or
links contained in this book may have changed since publication and
may no longer be valid. The views expressed in this work are solely those
of the author and do not necessarily reflect the views of the publisher,
and the publisher hereby disclaims any responsibility for them.

The author of this book does not dispense medical advice or prescribe the use
of any technique as a form of treatment for physical, emotional, or medical
problems without the advice of a physician, either directly or indirectly. The
intent of the author is only to offer information of a general nature to help
you in your quest for emotional and spiritual well-being. In the event you use
any of the information in this book for yourself, which is your constitutional
right, the author and the publisher assume no responsibility for your actions.

ISBN: 978-1-4525-3560-9 (sc)
ISBN: 978-1-4525-3562-3 (hc)
ISBN: 978-1-4525-3561-6 (e)

Library of Congress Control Number: 2011908903

Printed in the United States of America

Balboa Press rev. date: 06/14/2011

ABOUT THE AUTHOR

I began a habit which transformed into an addiction in writing poetry at the age of 11. It was another way to express who I am, and what I was feeling at the time.

Unlike an ordinary child reading a bed time story before bed, I'd have my pen and paper ready to be filled with unconditional words that represented how my day was spent. A lot of my writing was influenced by other people's lives which had an effect of what I felt and how I wrote my poetry. It was as though I walked a mile in each of their shoes.

A lot of my poetry is not only based on my personal life but the people that I have seen experience their own aspect of life.

Sarah Chemaissem 19/1/1987

PURPOSE OF LOVE AND SUCCESS

Some times we say goodbye to the person we love without wanting to. Though that doesn't mean that we've stopped loving them we've just stopped to care. Sometimes goodbye is a painful way to say I love you because we don't know any other way to express it, it's not so good with the outcome, but our emotions take the better of us and we tend to loose control.

One of the hardest things you'll ever have to do is stop loving someone because they've stopped loving you. But you know what they say "It's better to have love and lost, then to have never loved at all".

Love may sometimes be painful in many ways, but it's worth the while in end, you'll always have that beautiful memory of the past, something so deep so sensual and soothing. Just remembering the first eye contact which followed with the roses sent to work, or the walk on the beach, even the laugh over something so meaningless but yet so loving and special at the time. All this comes with the memories of love, do you remember that butterfly feeling when ever he/she just held your hand, or that hot flush when he/she whispered something special in your ear. Or even the song you sang thinking its eternal whilst jumping with excitement and singing though its meant to be.

All these memories should be cherished and held close to you. It is one of the best's chapters of your life and something you can tell you children and grandchildren.

When you try your best to make things work in any sector and never give up, it will work to your favor in the end. Also keep in mind in a relationship there is always one person working harder than the other to make it work, but if that person wasn't there, were do you think the relationship would be? Honestly? If you are both hot headed or stubborn at times, it might be caused from work, family, finances etc. Can you imagine where the relationship would be? There won't be a relationship at all.

It takes time to change but perseverance will get you there, don't ever give up on yourself, because when you do, the people around you will too. Keep in mind were only human and we all make mistakes but the successful humans are the ones that never give up, they strive and strive for more. Don't ever let the pain and hurt get you down put that band aid on and walk through it. You are the only person who can succeed; you're the key to your happiness, love and success.

In order to be happy to the fullest try some of these pointers below...

Live with integrity

Always be true to yourself. Take pride in whatever you do. Be proud of who you are and what you represent. Accept others with all their flaws. Show compassion and goodwill to others. Be dignified. Lead a life of purpose and be proud of your values.

Show gratitude

Show gratitude and say thank-you to the people who have helped you along the way. Send a handwritten letter to someone who has touched you. Call up a friend or loved one and tell them how much they mean to you. Compliment a colleague or business associate on a job well done. Show people you appreciate and care about them. Acts of kindness cost nothing but mean everything.

Be passionate

Show passion in everything you do. Let it show in your body language, in your smile, in your voice. Let your eyes sparkle. Let the world see and hear your enthusiasm and let it feel your passion. Before you go to bed your body will feel at ease and content.

Dedicate quality time

Life is so precious; make the most of each and every day. Rise early, spend some quality time by yourself as well as with those you care about. Go for a walk, workout, read a book. Value not only the time you spend with your loved ones, but also the time you spend with you. It will make you feel more relaxed.

Don't be anxious with small stuff

Let go of the little things you can't control. Don't take yourself so seriously. Recognise that perfection isn't always the only option. Don't let life's imperfections bother you. Lighten up and see the funny side of things when they go wrong. Be tolerant, smile and most of all don't waste your energies on the small stuff, it's not worth your time.

Last but not least...

Challenge yourself

Have a clear vision and focus on what you want to achieve, set a time frame. Challenge yourself to be the best at all times, *"even if people get you down"*. Visualise what you want to accomplish and then go for it *"See it and dream it in your mind"*. Write down your goals *"stick it on the back of your door"* have a plan of action, and never doubt yourself as you will be successful. Keep in mind you will need to fail 50% more before you become successful.

"One who feeds shall receive nothing but good fortune"

SOMETHING TO LIVE BY...

♥ ♥ ♥

When you say, "I love you", mean it
Believe in love at first site
Remember that great love and
great achievements involve great risk
Open your arms to change, but don't let go of your values
Give people more than they expect and do it cheerfully
Pray. There's immeasurable power in it
Trust in God but lock your car
Spend some time alone, it will give you relief
When you say, 'I'm sorry', look the person in the eye
Share your knowledge. It's a way to achieve immortality
Judge your success by what you had to give up
in order to receive it
If you make a lot of money, put it to use helping others while
you are living. That is wealth's greatest satisfaction
When you realize you've made a mistake,
take immediate steps to correct it
Call your mother every week, you will be rewarded
Say 'bless you' when you hear someone sneeze
Never laugh at anybody's dream
Write it on your heart the word IMPOSSIBLE says IM POSSIBLE
Don't believe all you hear, spend all you have,
nor sleep all you want.
Once a year, go someplace you've never been before
Remember that not getting what you want is
sometimes a stroke of luck
Live a good, honorable life. Then when you get older and
think back, you'll get to enjoy it a second time.
Remember that your character is your destiny

LOST IN A DREAM

♥ ♥ ♥

I feel so lost in this world
I'm here but my soul is else where.
This life has changed who I was and who ill be
It's quite scary and all strange to me
My poetry is dead, my heart is cold
My life is empty, and I'm so darn COLD
I don't know who I've become
I want to wake up to view the old me
But how can I?
While I'm still living in a dream

WALK WITH ME

♥ ♥ ♥

Walk with me, the path of life
To explore every bend of the road
Enjoy with me the beauty of life,
Along it's wonderful way.

Find comfort with me, in each others arms
When grief crosses our path
Find with me, in each others strength
When despair lies in wait

Laugh with me, a single true laugh
To enlighten another's distress
Cry with me, a single true tear,
To understand true happiness

Cherish with me, the wonders of life,
As they need to be preserved
Rejoice with me, in the mysteries,
Of what is yet to be

Find peace with me, in each others souls,
When the world has gone insane
Find love with me, in each others hearts,
Until this life has fulfilled

And when the path comes to an end
I hope we can say from within
We've known the beauty of true love,
Our love came from within.

A SPECIAL WORLD

♥ ♥ ♥

A special world for you and me
A special bond one cannot see
It wraps us up in its cocoon
And holds us fiercely in its womb

Its fingers spread like fine spun gold
Gently nestling us to the fold
Like silken thread it holds us fast
Bonds like this are meant to last

And though at times a thread may break
A new one forms its wake
To bind us closer and keep us strong
In a special world, where we belong

WHAT HE'S DONE FOR ME

♥ ♥ ♥

For so long I've been lonely
Drowning in my tears
No one there to listen
Or help me face my deepest fears
No one there to shelter me
From this world we call home,
No one showed me rainbows
Every time I saw rain.
No one there to give a damn
About my broken heart,
No one to pick up the pieces
Every time I fell apart.
But finally someone came along
And took the time to share,
All the hurt and pain, even despair
That I tried so hard not to show
He took the time to realize
How much I've had to pay,
For every time I gave of me
There was something taken away.
He took the time to look inside
This heart as cold as stone,
He found that there was something there
No one else had ever known
He found what I'd been hiding
Brought it out to show the world,
That there was so much love inside
Of such a lonely girl
He knew what I was feeling

So he set my mind at ease,
Then he did the impossible
He gave my soul to me.
So now I'm going to take this time
To give 'thanks' for all his done,
And hope he knows I love him more
Then life or anyone

NOT MINE

Words cannot explain
Feelings so strong inside
It makes me want to cry (deep down inside)
I am laying down here
I feel you all around
Your touch so gentle
Your lips against mine
Faster and faster my heart beats
As you become mine
Realizing I am not alone
I try to let go
But there's something about you
I still do not know
I turn around and walk straight by
While you lay there
Thinking your mine...

REALITY

I look you in the eyes
Thinking its all divine
Not realizing reality
Has its cruelty on us all
Thinking it will pass by like a raw
But now I've come to realize
That maybe we weren't meant to be
Harder and harder, A day goes by
Not thinking of you is such a lie
Knowing we cant be,
Is something you cannot explain to me.
Living a fantasy, is just the way it's meant to be

NOT MEANT TO BE

♥ ♥ ♥

Minding my own business
As days go by,
Thinking to myself
Its nothing but a dream
Feeling for someone
Is nothing but another day, swift with the wind
And the air we breathe
Is just a simple thing
Now you here, my world has changed
I breathe the air each passing day
Looking forward for another say
I feel as though we were meant to be
Not knowing its not up to me
I feel as though you're here forever and only for me
Not knowing I can't have you
For the reasons to be,
As my desires come closer to thee,
Feelings like these all have to go
But wanting you is all ill ever know
As I lay bleeding to thee
Minding my own business
It just wasn't meant to be

WHERE DO WE GO?

♥ ♥ ♥

Today has come
Yesterday is gone
Waiting for tomorrow
Knowing our feelings but not knowing how strong
So puzzled for the day
When it will all show,
Knowing we can't be is the cruelest thing to know
Not knowing which step to take
Makes me only plee
I don't want to be played
It's all happened once before
Before you know I'll be gone
So what are you waiting for?
My heart was meant for you
But I guess it just wasn't meant to be.

TOGETHER BECOME WE

Falling in love with someone is trusting thee
But falling in love with you is what you do to me
Your sweet touch has captured my heart
Your laughter to thee apart, the smile that melts me inside
Within those gorgeous eyes, I can't wait to see thee
As you come closer and I become we

ONE

Beneath these covers is hidden
Something so sweet, so deep
Something I can only imagine
You're all I see, your touch so near
Softness of your skin I long for dear
Sharing one passion, our world turns to one
Heart pounding to your soft touch
My world is spinning, as you explore me inside
Feeling I cannot clarify
Blood rushing fast, my breath becomes deeper
Our bodies electrified with passion
As you complete the quest of our love
Fate has brought us together
As we become in one world
Lips caressing as we turn to ONE!

"Love is discovered by our ignorance of life"

LOVE OR NOT?

— ♥ ♥ ♥ —

Words cannot describe
How I truly feel,
Nothing is more insane than not being with you
Your eyes say it all
Filled with passion, desire
And nothing more,
Just take my hand and lead the way
Please don't go astray, choose our destined path
That will not move us apart
Please take my hand and I shall make you the happiest man
I promise with all I have you will be pleased,
Just take a chance and give our love a try.
So will you lead the way
Shall I turn away?

TRAGIC

Tragic life
Tragic world
Tragic moments
Tragic me
That's all I know
All I want is you
But knowing, I can't have you
Kills me more inside
Pressure from everyone
I've had enough
Why is this happening to me
Isn't it enough
It's not fair, what have I done to deserve
All this mistress in my life
When things get you down
Sometimes there are no turning backs
All I can think about is you and your touch
Besides mine, your eyes that stare and oh that's so divine.
You're a mistress that floats in my dreams
You're a gift that I can not keep
Your there for only one person which isn't me
I stand here as my is tragic and there's nothing more

SUFFERING

You're not the person I thought you were
You're something from my worst nightmares
Never thought it could come to life
Never thought I could detect it on my own
It was hard challenging and unbearable
Every time I hear your name it turns my stomachs
How can so much hatred form for only one?
It deludes my mind, overwhelms my heart
Just to think of you, and being apart...
So I write this to you today with vain
To confess my deepest and outmost honest thoughts of you
Now I've realized the person I thought
once I knew has left in shame.

WITH YOU

Days of sunshine
Days of rain
Days of disaster
In many ways
Days of laughter
Days of joy
But days without you
Is not a day at all

MISSING YOU

Busy day
Busy life
Busy week
Is what I like
Hair all done
Money prepared
Shopping spree
Is what I can bare
Love and romance
Not on the list
But you my dear is what I miss

THINKING

♥ ♥ ♥

Thinking of you as the day drifts by
Why are you still on my mind?
Working to late
It's so busy today
Love, warmth and passion
Is what I feel
You are the one I call in the night
I love you dearly, can't you tell?
My love for you will never subside
As the days go by, thinking...
I can't seem to get you off my mind

LOVE

Love is thought to be something special within
It's so special that you have embraced it into your arms
Love is thought to be something profound
It's so profound that wisdom begins to embrace me
Your love for me is so unconditional so deep and pure
Love is thought to be selfless, fulfilling and eternal
Love is what I feel deeply for you

WISHING YOU NEAR

All but a dream
Lying in the dark
Something is not clear
Is it from the past
Here I am
Buts what's above
Were not alone as I sense your touch
The softness of you lips
A glimpse of your heart
I lay in the dark
As it all comes to clear
You're only but a dream
Wishing you near

FANTASY

I was sort of hoping
That you would come along
Like a dream come to life
Or a melody to a song

Setting me free
From this chamber I call home
Changing my life forever
It will not be the same

This fantasy was real
Before I knew your name
And now that I have found you
My feelings have changed

So pardon if I look at you
Forgive me if I stare
I dreamt this dream before
I saw you standing there.

Finally, you're here standing
Like an answer to a prayer
With the melody to a song

WHAT I LOVE ABOUT YOU

♥ ♥ ♥

I love the way you look at me
Your love so tender and true
I love the way you kiss me
Your lips so soft and smooth

I love the way you make me smile
And the ways you show you care
I love the way you say "I love you"
And that you're always there

I love the way you touch me
Forever sending chills down my spine
I love that you are with me
And glad I can call you mine

WITHOUT YOU

This world is empty
This world is blue
This world is useless without you
Left here in gloom
Grey is all I see, grey is all I feel
My world has come to an end
Without a doubt, you stole my heart
And returned it blue
Sitting here lost without you

"Love has such meaning that you cannot explore
its great wonders in less you've lived it"
"Love is empty, love is blue, love has no feelings, so don't you!"

YOU'RE EYES

Sitting beside the coffee table,
As the music is playing
Relaxing on this recliner, I couldn't help but begin to say
My pen has taken over this page
My thoughts can't keep up anymore
My heart has began to reside
Of all the past we've over come
A love as strong as this, is one we cannot hide
A love as deep as this, is one we cannot despise
A light shines so deep within your heart
My senses come to life
A light of happiness glows only when I look into your eyes.

MY LIFE

The foundation of our love
Is so strong that wind cannot move it if it tried.
I'm so glad your presence we share every night
Your eyes have captured me from the very start
You smile warms every corner of my soul
Your voice is like a dazzling mountain stream
Which flows into my heart
Your walk, you hair
Your hands I crave to touch
Your arms I long to have around my neck
As you pull me close to your warmth
Most of all everything you are
Changed the way I feel about my life
For that I adore you

WALKED AS ONE

My heart is pounding
Racing to reach my breath
Just in time, he turns and stares
Lusciously inviting, with his seductive eyes
My eyes soften to touch his skin
Moving towards me, my body begins to quiver
My heart at my feet as heat waves begin to strike
Turning the other way, hand by hand
As we both walked as one.

SLEEPLESS NIGHTS

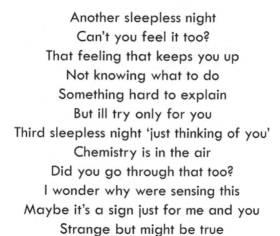

Another sleepless night
Can't you feel it too?
That feeling that keeps you up
Not knowing what to do
Something hard to explain
But ill try only for you
Third sleepless night 'just thinking of you'
Chemistry is in the air
Did you go through that too?
I wonder why were sensing this
Maybe it's a sign just for me and you
Strange but might be true

TYPICAL

I thought you were my angle sent from heavens sky
I thanked god for your presence but now I wonder why
U took your bow and arrow and aimed it to my heart
You let it rip through my soul and left me torn apart...
It made me wonder what went wrong
I loved you without doubt,
But I figured out above all things
You're just a typical male!

STILL NOT FOUND

Can you feel that strong weight upon your chest?
Heaviness clashing your head
The tension that causes no rest
Weakness in your knees, leaving you to fall
Sadness hidden underneath, forming a scar so deep
Looking into my eyes, sadness and despise
Reaching out to you, as you turned and left me in the blue
My world begins to spin, into a endless twist
Round and round, I begin to fall
Slowly slipping down to the ground
Shattered to pieces, still not found!

SEIZING TO EXIST

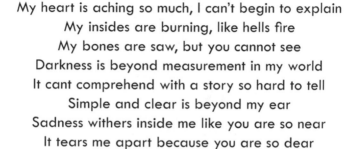

My heart is aching so much, I can't begin to explain
My insides are burning, like hells fire
My bones are saw, but you cannot see
Darkness is beyond measurement in my world
It cant comprehend with a story so hard to tell
Simple and clear is beyond my ear
Sadness withers inside me like you are so near
It tears me apart because you are so dear
My passion in life has slowly drifted with the wind
Only tears is what you can see
My passion, desire, devotion to life
Now only seizes to EXIST!

WHERE DO WE GO?

Today has come
Yesterday is gone
Waiting for tomorrow
Knowing our feelings but not knowing how strong
So puzzled for the day
When it will all reveal
Knowing we cannot be is the, cruelest you know
Not knowing which step to take
Makes me only plea
I don't want to be played
Its happened once, and no more
Before you know ill be gone
My heart is aching and yearning for a glimpse
So, I guess it just wasn't meant to be!

TOGETHER BECOME WEI

Falling in love is trusting
But falling in love with you is what you do to me
Your sweet touch has captured my heart
Your laughter will not part,
Your smile which lingers me inside
Your dazzling eyes, I just can not wait to see
As you come closer and I become WE

TRUE LOVE

♥ ♥ ♥

From all those stormy days
And strongest rain,
You picked me up from all the rest,
Helped me through this awful test

You showed me hope, when I was down
You held me high when all was lost
Filled my heart with love and joy

You showed me how to be
To be someone with a stronger will
To see I'm not alone
Though it was hard on both of us
You didn't give me up!
You made me see that I was once found
That love is true and never blind

My life had no direction
A road of uncertainty
But now we have a journey
Together you and me

I thank my lucky stars
And god from heaven above
For my heart and soul could never
Feel the impact of true love.
Until you came along

How wonderful that I can share
A love like this with you!

LOVE OR NOT?

♥ ♥ ♥

Words cannot describe
How I truly feel inside
Nothing is more insane than not being with you
Your eyes say it all
Filled with passion, desire
And nothing more
I promise I will give you all I have
And much much more
Just take my hand and lead the way
Please don't go astray,
Choose our destined path
By taking my hand and allowing me
To make you the happiest man
I promise with all I have, you will be pleased
Take the chance, give our love a try
So the question still lies?
Will you lead the way?
Or Shall I turn away?

NOT MEANT TO BE

Minding my own business
As days go by
Thinking to myself
Its nothing but a dream
Feelings for someone
Is nothing but another day swifed with wind
And the air we breath
Is just a simple thing
Now you're here, my world has changed
I breath the air each passing day
Looking forward to another day
I feel as though were meant to be
Not knowing its not up to me
Feeling as though you're here forever
And only meant for me
Not knowing I can't have you
For reasons to be
As my desires come closer
Feelings like these all begin to fade
Wanting you is all ill ever know
As I lye bleeding
Minding my own business
It just wasn't meant to be!

REALITY!

♥ ♥ ♥

I look you in the eyes
Thinking all is so divine
Not realizing reality
Has its cruelty on us all
Thinking it will pass by
Now I've come to realize
Were not meant to be
Harder and harder my days go by
Not thinking of you is such a lie
Fate has taken its toll
And leaving us apart
Knowing this is something you cannot explain
So living a fantasy,
Is just the way it's meant to be!

YOU'RE SUPPORT

♥ ♥ ♥

A burden,
A feeling so strong
Holds on for a minute
Maybe even longer
Struggles as I get older
Finding my way
Realizing my dreams
As you try to destroy me,
Let me be, let me go!
I promise you, you won't be dissatisfied
But realize I have my dreams
And this I need on my own
I don't need your help
But I just need you there!

GODS ANSWER!

Why does it hurt so bad to lose something I never had?
I now can see who he truly was
Blinded by love isn't that what they say?
It hid the smallest of secretes, that he denied.
6 months have passed, since I last saw his face
Memories of smallest moments, aren't close to fade away
Something tells me his not coming back.
Even though there wasn't much between us
But something just kept me looking back
It might have been that smile, which teased me
It might have been his hands, drawing me closer
It might have been his eyes, which hypnotized me
Either way he definitely fooled ME!
Not so innocent as I thought
Not the honesty that I bought
Not so charming, with looks so deceiving
That took my breath away

I prayed to god every night
Night after night just to bring you closer to me,
But all was seen and heard, silence was only found
I guess he had other plans set out for me
Taking me months to realize, without an appetite
Realizing my bones came to bore
God grant me the courage to change the things I can,
The patience to accept the things I can't,
And the wisdom to know that great things lie ahead for me

Nothing was left to say
God has answered my prayers
An experience of something new,
A test to see my faith within
He didn't want me to get hurt any more
But only to experience the unknown,
And thank him for what his given me
By getting closer to his presence...

"One who doesn't feed is nothing but greed"

WITHOUT YOU

♥ ♥ ♥

This world is empty
This world is blue
This world is useless without you
Left here in gloom
Grey is all see, grey is all I feel
My world has come to an end
Without a word or intent
You stole my heart
And returned it blue
Now I'm sitting here
Feeling lost without you!

THE END OF A DREAM

Rushing through the clock of dawn,
Reaching the journey where he awaits only to
find another to love.
Slow tear drop rolls down her face
In silence not a word was spoken
Surrounding her the joy of others
Endlessly alone in her room
Closed windows in a darkened room,
Glooming of red, no passion to see
Finding her self alone,
with no redemption of what has happened.
Sadness, sorrow was only felt
Feelings disappearing from the side of light
Only to find herself breaking with tears
No words left to say, explaining her pain

Covered in silk, lying alone in satin sheets
Slowly her eye lids begin to close
Realizing all the pain that was always there
Leaving her now alone
Suddenly he reaches to address her once again
Secretly moving away from him
He surrounds her with joy, to feel the love they once shared
Silently moving back, from what was once there
Pleading for forgiveness, please take me back
Refusing the plea, caressing her skin and weakening her knees
Pleading for the chance that she refused to begin

Laying there, finding her self loved once
by the man, she called life
Rapped with passion that surrounds her spirit with love
Endlessly thinking of what has become of a lifeless bore

I DON'T KNOW

I don't know who to trust
Everything seems to fall to dust
Where do I go, when all my doors are closed?
What does this mean?
I've lost everything within my dreams
Why do I give in?
Perhaps it's harder resisting
I don't know when ill move on..
I've felt so empty since you're gone
I don't know how ill move on
My happiness was so long ago

*"Love has such meaning that you cannot
explore its great wonders unless you've lived it"*

LOVE THAT DIDN'T MOVE

♥ ♥ ♥

Their I sat writing poems of love for you
Hands tremble, just thinking of you
Heart burning deep down inside
The day I don't see you, is the day I die
Leaving me standing, begging for more
Dreams faded, through beings core
My hearts flame, turned so cold

I wrote to you all my love
I wrote to you with my tears that I've missed you
I wrote to you from my heart (that burned)
I wrote my mistakes (and how they hurt you)
I wrote my life, future and history for you

So I say...

If my tears didn't move you
If my words didn't bring you
If my love didn't capture you
Forget everything I've just told you
Forget all the poems I wrote to you
Forget all the tears I cried for you
Forget all the love I gave you
Forget all the ways I looked at you
Forget what I could have given you

Just remember you did mistakes
Remember how you used me 'and I forgave you'
Remember what you've said about me
Remember the way you stared at me
Remember what you've promised me
Remember everything you've told me
Remember the way my touch moved you
Remember your heart racing when I held you

LISTEN TO THAT VOICE

♥ ♥ ♥

Can you hear that voice?
Calling out your name at night
Touching your heart, softly inside
Breathing heavenly into your soul
Drifting further in the cold
Feeling your warmth beneath the sheets
Whispering voices down so deep

Can you hear that voice?
Wishing you near,
Gently touching your skin
To see it's just a dream

Can you hear that voice?
Screaming out with fear
Seeking help 'eternally'

That's what I hear calling
Through the night
Strangely feeling what he can feel
Souls so close, it trembles deep within
I feel you, I feel everything
I hear you, I hear everything
Just if you knew, it would be clear
Love comes deep within,
Setting our souls free
Together we can BE!

SOULS INTERTWINE

My thoughts, mind and soul are miles away
Thinking of you, my mind gets out of control
So many feelings run deep within
Wishing you near, touching your skin
Crying out to feel your gentle touch
Upon my cheek whispering softly in my ear
The things I long to hear
My soul cries out in vain
Only to see you again
Missing you is all I do
My thoughts, mind and soul are miles away
All I wish is for another day
A day were I can see you once again
To feel your warmth that calls me in the night
Reaching out to me, as our souls intertwine

"Love is empty, love is blue,
love has no feelings 'so don't you'"

PRECIOUS GIFT

So many thoughts, I can't keep up on this page
My pen tries to catch up to my feelings
I long to say, my heart skips a beat
When I hear you name, moments fly when were together
Years go by without you near
My soul deepens to feel your touch
And smell you near
Your eyes that sparkle only to me
Have captured my soul, so deep within
If only you knew what you mean to me
Life is a fairytale since you walked in
I'm floating with angels in clouds I've never seen
You have captured my heart, and brightened my years
Days without you are so empty
When I hear your voice I'm reborn again
To you I'm grateful,
I've found my fairytale that once was a dream
Now its reality that will always hold you dear
You have enriched my life, so to you I'll always be faithful,
For you are, a precious gift!

DREAM

Can you feel that gentle breeze?
Under the covered sheets?
Paralyzing your body within skin so deep
It deepens as you breathe
Taking over and letting me in
You begin to tremble, not from fear
Trembling to the sound of my sigh
Caressing your skin,
So soft and gentle, conveying your insecurities
You no longer fear
Bringing us closer, only to wake
It's all but a dream

AS ONE

You're so close, don't let me go
I'm in love, to you I say so
You've taken my hand
Showed me life, meaning to words
With out you I will die
Reborn through sunshine's end
Magical to worlds end
Something I haven't seen, has captured me
I'm in so deep, no looking back
You've taken my hand
Somewhere nice, this is a fantasy land
My feelings can't be explained, it's you I need
You've taken my woos, replaced them with hope
My life has just began
A journey together AS ONE!

WE WALK AS ONE

Passion desire runs through my skin
Whispers that hollow when you're near
My passion is yet to begin
You've whispered words I long to hear
Brought me closer, now you're so dear
Words cannot describe these feelings, passion, and desire
That runs deep within my veins
To feel your touch
Forever so you will stay
Stay close to my heart
Stay close to me
My body yearns to feel your skin
On the softness of your touch
My body yearns for more
Take me in your arms
Hold me tight
Forever more make sweet love to me
Ill hold you close, taking my hand
We walk as one

*"Touch of your hand,
made me feel spontaneous and sent me to glory my heart
sunk and my body went into heat for love, feelings my
body only explains to me"*

TROUBLED LOVE

Troubled people, troubled world
What are these people coming too
A minute happy, a minute sad
There is no end, just keeps dragging on
I love him clearly, with all my heart
He sees it is me, without a doubt
Troubles have brought us down
We try to talk, but left there with a frown
Im sick of this, im sick of this world
Tell me why? Why is this all happening
All I do is cry deep down
Only to find my self saddened
My soul shattered
My world so empty
Left with this frown
What have you done
What have I done wrong?
Answer my plee
I'm not staying for long!
You both have problems
Why get us involved
You've discovered this matter
In hands untold
I give you all my goodbyes
Its time for me to go
I'll see you in another lifetime
That holds us so!

WHY?

Why did it have to be so hard?
Why did it have to hurt so much?
That I wanted you so bad
When were you goner realize all the love I had for you
It just won't go away
You might not no
I might not show
But no one else will do
If you only knew
The love I had for you

SILLY ME

♥ ♥ ♥

I opened up and let you in
U promised it wasn't a sin
You broke my heart into a hundred pieces
And walked away...
You begged for a chance
Which I gave
Instead you broke my heart again
This time you took a piece with you
And never gave it back!
I'm longing for that piece as it
Will only make me complete!
What a fool was I?
Given it to you to begin with...
Silly me!

"The worst way to miss someone is to be sitting right beside them knowing you can't have them"

CURSED

You stole my heart
From the moment I saw you
And smashed it into two
You traded me for a person
Which I cannot start to explain
You will not find someone like me
Or find the love I showed you
You have been cursed on,
Not so much a lucky man
For you don't deserve my love
That possesses within,
This love will be given to somebody
So special that you cannot see!
As for my heart can heal
And re-love again a man that possesses me!

LOVE

Here I stand
Strong and tall
I look near
But don't look at all
You surround me with joy,
Love to fulfill.
I look around me and wish to reveal
This precious feeling moving me to you
Wishing you near, as whispers follow
Your whisper nears as my body shivers
I look to you glancing at me
As we both fall in love...